# DON'T LOOK BACK

# Also by Dabney Stuart

**POETRY**

*The Diving Bell* (1966)
*A Particular Place* (1969)
*The Other Hand* (1974)
*Round and Round* (1977)
*Rockbridge Poems* (1981)
*Common Ground* (1982)

**FOR CHILDREN**

*Friends of Yours, Friends of Mine* (1974)

**CRITICISM**

*Nabokov: The Dimensions of Parody* (1978)

# DON'T LOOK BACK

Poems by DABNEY STUART

Louisiana State University Press

Baton Rouge and London    1987

Designer: Albert Crochet
Typeface: Palatino
Typesetter: G&S Typesetters, Inc.
Printer: Thomson-Shore, Inc.
Binder: John H. Dekker & Sons, Inc.

Grateful acknowledgment is made to the following publications,
where some of these poems originally appeared: *Crescent Review,
Denver Quarterly, Harvard Magazine, Kentucky Poetry Review,
Memphis State Review, National Forum, New Virginia Review, North
American Review, Ohio Review, Poetry, Poetry East, Prairie Schooner,
Publications of the Arkansas Philological Association, Southern Poetry
Review, Southern Review, Tar River Poetry, Tendril, Virginia
Quarterly Review*

I am grateful to Washington and Lee University for a leave of
absence and a summer grant that helped me find time to work
on many of the poems in this book, especially the longer ones. I
am also grateful to the National Endowment for the Arts for a
Literary Fellowship that was invaluable.

LIBRARY OF CONGRESS CATALOGING-IN-PUBLICATION DATA

Stuart, Dabney, 1937–
    Don't look back.

    I. Title.
PS3569.T8D6 1986        811'.54        86-18606
ISBN 0-8071-1374-3
ISBN 0-8071-1384-0 (pbk.)

*for Sandra*

# Contents

SIX

# DON'T LOOK BACK

## Talking to the Small Voice

Before he became the smoke
from his own fire

he turned toward the small rain
still falling

in his childhood,
and the child he was

standing in it, and said
*Come warm yourself with me.*

*Together*
*we may stop burning.*

 # ONE

## Bound Up

Men must have seemed an alien species to you,
And not because of their dumb organ either—
Roots are roots—but because the courtly procedure
Tilted the world from your feet, defining
Happiness as elevation, a laced bodice:
Airs to be put on, borne up under.

How did you live so long up there, with such pressure?
Once upon a time is never, but no one told you.
When you found out, you heard the world's splintering
As the music of your own lost chances
Reduced to one peace. Rest in it, first lady:
Desire was no likelier than the evasions of desire.

## Once More for My Lady

### 1

No matter how gently, with what suspended
fierceness, from however deep a well
of passion longing to be lifted, oblivious,

                                        no

matter how gently you touch a woman,

if she does not wish to be touched
or, wishing, does not wish yours, does not begin
to turn away
from the grottoed vista of her self
                              toward
the future hovering between
your barely perceptible hand and her flesh,

then it is no different from brute ice
laid on with mason's trowel.

2

                              How often,
most loved woman, did you turn
*your* husband into a bricklayer?
                              Did he become
just another man who gave occasion
for your fondest ceremonies—the least
of which got you children—and then receded?
Those raucous energies I remember
echoing from the grease pit of his boat—
was it you who compressed them finally
into his tinkling glass, and the raw curse
of his last, contagious years?
                              What did you bring him,
bring him to?—twin questions
between which his life, like beaten metal,
thinned inexorably for fifty years.
                              When you saw him
stricken, desolate, supine, mindless,
his days dribbling through the slack lips,
did the image come unbidden
of him young again, at no one's mercy
then but yours? Did he
lead you far enough out of your self once,
or enough, to make you remember now,
honoring him unknowing with that palimpsest
grief no grave posture satisfies?
Did you reach out to the image?

3

Your laced aloofness straitened your husband.

To me, who didn't know the stakes yet, it seemed
exemplary, the only way things were.

Before I could
imagine sex, conceive
a trite fold, or probe
or mazy wander
in any lady's chamber,
                              you set out
these determinations in the room I slept in:

a crazed
porcelain ewer, off-white, a matching
basin and, under the bed, chamber pot
with its cold lip, a cut-
glass decanter webbed
with starbursts of spirits, the ghosts
of spirits, crystal snowcrystal,
crystalized camphor—
                              even now you present to me
in dreams
pitcher, bowl, pot, decanter,
set on a plateau of veined marble
you bear before you, raised,
a salver.

You bow.

Your white hair descends about you, robing.

4

Heartbeat, what else could you be?
An interlude at the grand hotel,
throb for a passing drummer, high-C
at a woman's club solo, slow belle
of the ball in a pressed book

of scraps and tag-ends? No, of
course not, not when the first look
to the last spasm and crack of love
was one long portrait to be tested
against the future: a full career,
a conception. You never rested
from it until, near eighty, your
own death started to craze
the canvas, mute its colors, score
those old configurations, amaze
the horizon, me, everyone—you.
You weren't immune. How simple. Life,
and the art it conjured up, became
the last thing you'd expect, an empty frame.
Too neat, too simple? No. For you,
though more than mother, widow, wife,
and type of these, lived to discover
you were also fiercely less.
Before it was over
you had nothing left to bless

and blessed it.

5

These are the desolate, sad days,
when the crow sits on the fencepost
cawing his gross syllable

and we stuff our dumb fingers
into the wounds of the planet
to prove it palpable, present, real.

The air in this paneled den thickens
with memory and dust:
where I sit, the shaft of sunlight

prods my shins and the low table,
the base of the crazed spinet;
I hear the crow's flight diminish

6

his long-winded spiel.
To increase distance, the poet says,
is to decrease pain. Maybe. But the singers

of darkness know the past quickens
when you wait on it, attending,
and know the dead never finish

asking their questions of your life.
I open the window.
                    Your life
        is over, grandmother: it was

        almost as ordered as these stanzas
        are, more obvious and severe
        in its gentility. But the ending

        didn't fit, that cancerous claw
        dragging and digging at your teeth
        until it tore away the whole jaw.

        The doctors could stuff that with gauze,
        drug it dumb, but the raw ghost
        that burned in the char of your eyes

        responded to nothing but death.
        Through those last long weeks
        I kept seeing

        the trenchant jaw and austere cheekbone
        of your marvelous face,
        an immortal profile, cause

        and brunt of love, the priming face—
        kept seeing burn in your fierce eyes
        far off that desperate ghost, as though

        I looked through binoculars
        the wrong way. In another age
        that would be an image

for the depths of your soul. All I know
is that you stared through me, neither slept
nor spoke, and then died, your scars

intact.
            This room, this window, this light
scar me now. A long life wants crust.
Those last mute weeks peeled hers to the quick

and she willed me the vision. We give
what we can, all right, and I live
with this, finding it neither trick

nor secret, finding not truth
inscrutable, but the ways
we manage it. She left me dust

and a wrack of light to float
it in, a trapped shadow in the shape
of a bird to roost on it and bring

forth from its exorbitant throat
the sound of grief
in the form of celebration.


## Taking the Wheel

1.

It's you and me again, Duststroke,
Curseworld. Until you spoke
to me in the midst of my own words
it had seemed a peaceful decade
between us. Now the old wind swells;
its movement in my throat, on my forehead,
reminds me we have been standing in it
together all this time without reprieve:
silence is no less a place than any other.

I know what your life came to,
how it ended: the splitbrain wrack
addling on the pillow beside your mouth,
the damned lock growing in your jaw.
*God damn it to hell* you had kept shouting,
repeating your last words for three years
infinitely, as if speech itself
is a rock we break
against, or a passage with frozen gates
we enter, and enter, until we are stoven in.
*Welcome* you tell me now, your voice as clear
in my head as a buoy's bell in raw fog.

I could sail halfway around the world
in a closed cabin with the shades drawn, and learn
as much as you ever taught me about death.
It's taken me this long to see that as your gift.
You made me heir to the intricate fierce spaces
which lead only to each other, and are called life;
and the curse you laid like a rope in my hand
leads over the side again, disappears
in the dark reaches where it's all one,
where it begins.
                    The first time I tried
to be fish
—finning wide-eyed through the drowning water,
happy to change my nature—
I never wanted to come back, give up that warm
release from everything, being all over.
But you pulled me out anyway, set me adrift
on the ground again, kicking and crying,
as if to say, *Shove off, it's not that easy.*

Now it appears I have to answer
the rope's pull again, follow it under
the maps, make up my mind, stand at the wheel
of this dustraft and dive.
                            I can
hear my sons
in the next room munching their sleep.
One of them turns, pulling his blanket

up over his backside; tomorrow is stacked
on their dressers, waiting to be put on.
Saving me for myself is a long pull
with no guarantee, grandfather, but together
I might find out what it means to accept and grieve.

2

My first son was born
twelve years on the wrong side
of your death. I am torn
to write this twenty-one
years in the same direction.

When I was nine
I rode a black horse free
on your small-time
beach carousel;
that fake calliope

music seemed to make
its circle go round,
my horse slide up
and down
on its golden pole: double mime
of this life.
                    Once, my stirrup
snapped while I stood
waving my hat to the crowd;
as I fell everything
tilted, the mad
music swarmed
over me, was nothing
to hold on to, my head
jarred on the bright wood.

The Rollercoaster you owned,
snaking its trite arcs,
and the sudden
Tunnel of Love diving
into the waves
of light, also took

me their tracked ways;
I have been thrown down
by their like, too.

My sons can be sure
to get all that and more
before they're through.

But they missed you.

3

The farthest reach
of my dark mind through darkness
is nothing to your sweet

grapple, the pull of your arms
through the long, viscid years.
You were the first

man in the world to know
how to make me welcome, to see
the wheel of light binding my head

and body in an early photograph
as me, a focus. Is that why
you hauled me out of the drowning water,

or is saving life
a reflex, like cursing?
Whatever it was that made you

bring me up,
I hear now beneath my words
your voice in my mind say *Welcome*.

*You will die as I died,*
*paralyzed, speech*
*stuck in your jaw like a cud,*

and know it to be fear
standing at the wheel and diving
at the same time, drowning in air.

## Meditation on My Grandfather's Lyric Names

*Duststroke*
> What paralysis rendered you
to the hospital sheet, letting you
neither sleep nor eat. And at home
the trail of fingertips
across the top of your chest of drawers,
the sunlight shafting the motes
in your empty bedroom: dust
of hours and breath, a map into which we are drawn,
the air of our travel.

*Curseworld*
> An imperative first, and enough life
to see around it: no delusions
about a cruise to far places, or wonder drugs,
as anything but a postponement;
> > then
a noun, a place through which we occur
together, some of us choosing
eventually to continue: a touchstone
of the drifter, a measure
of speech, and not the only
accomplishment we may pass on to our sons.

 **TWO**

## The Girl of My Dreams

How she would welcome my hands
into her body. The beat of her heart
depended on the skill of my massage!
Evenings after work
she would put on her best breasts
and sweater, float into my head
for a good feel. She would say
*I like your eyes on me*—even now
I sometimes mistake them for her nipples.
Her voice was always a combination
of my own and my mother's.
Such mutual devotion. By looking
through me she could create herself,
and I could take her with me unscathed
into the future, where
she would invariably choose me
over all comers. *There's no one else
but me* we would promise each other,
writing our names with chalk on the sidewalk.
When I played catch she would be thousands
cheering in the bleachers. Even now
I hear her calling *I am everywhere
you put yourself. Take me.*

## My Mother Announces She Is Pregnant

She is wearing a balloon.
Unbuttoning herself, she removes it
and ties it to the ceiling fixture
in my bedroom.
*For me?* I ask,
but she strokes it quietly,
then backs off and surveys it
from several angles, saying
*Yes. Oh, yes.*
*For a while there I wasn't sure*
*I could do better myself.*

The balloon expands
until the room is almost filled with it.
It presses me against the wall.
My bones liquify, I grow

shapeless. My knife
glitters on the dresser.
I reach to the end of myself
close my fingers around the handle
and sweep it through the air.

An explosion of nothing happens.

I feel the inside of my head
swell, hear fizz
from my mouth a breath
so long it stretches twenty or thirty years
into the future, a string even today
life floats at the end of.


## Finding My Face

"What have you done with it this time?"
my mother asks at breakfast.

"How can I carry on with my holy work
if you're not watching?"

"Oh, mother, or whoever you are,"
I write on a piece of paper.
"Give me your nipples and I will become a seer,
both male and female, like Teiresias;
with your nipples for eyes, I will weep
milk for the hungry children of the world.
I will raise the dead."

She rides the wave of my good humor
perfectly into the kitchen
where she performs the best pout of her career,
washing the dishes in her lower lip.

My father wipes up the last of his yolk
with a corner of toast and goes to work.
I trudge along after him,
watching the heavy buildings fill up
the empty air.

In the warehouse we discover my nose
deep in a hogshead of curing tobacco.
At first my father mistakes it for a raisin.
He hands it to me, tells me I'm lazy.
"You'll never make any money that way," he says,
but I sense a grudging admiration for something—
my shrewd choice of environment?
He pokes me in the ribs and gives me a wink
before vanishing behind an inventory graph.

It must be a game, I think,
the way they hide, the way they give
me the way they leave me.
Out in the street again
I see myself grow past the buildings
and write on the blue dome of sky, *Here
I am, ready or not.* I laugh,
feeling my head make its last
best opening to the world.

## 1943

I climb the stairs
into the long hall of my first day
at school.
All the teachers come
to attention outside the doors of their rooms.
In unison they step out
of their skirts and panties,
thrust themselves whole host forward
and call me to *Fire.*
"Yes ma'ams," I say
and fumble through my bag, giving
them a licorice stick, a ruler,
a lollypop, Hop Harrigan, the All-
American boy, a fountain
pen, the milk
concession in the cafeteria, almost
everything I
have. I expect them to writhe
against the wall, clutch
their hips and breasts, surrender,
but their hands flutter when they touch
themselves, they rub their knees
together, flecks of dry skin drift
to the marble floor. Still,
they plead *Never stop*
*doing this again until we tell*
*you to forever.*
After they put their clothes back
on and go into their rooms
their voices come
over the intercom system saying
*Good grades, good grades.*
We live like this for years,
recess to recess, and nobody ever
thinks to call it war.

## The Perfect Headache

Whenever I have the perfect headache
it clamps into the back of my eyeballs,
pitches camp in my eardrums;
from the base of my skull into the muscles
of my neck it sends down two iron pipes
in which the arrhythmic knocking announces
all my ancestors
have found a place to congregate
and lodge their complaints.
The sound of their little nation
waves in my cranium like a banner
that cracks in the softest breeze.
I want more than anything to join them,
to become the voice that finally splits
this incredible head
which let them in to begin with.
But they deny me.
No matter how often I salute
and point out how much they owe me
they go on with their storm as if I weren't there.
When they get tired, they assemble in rows
at the rims of my eyesockets
as in the hollow eyeholes of an idol.
Looking down on me they say variously
*How many times do we have to tell you?*
*The only way you'll get in here*
*and join the perfect image of yourself*
*we celebrate*
*is to stand up straight and be somebody*
*else.*

## Groundwork

The old woman who will let no one
love her is dreaming of me.

*Turn that thing off* she yells
to her husband, but it's mowing time,
he's deaf, and belongs
in another dream besides. She dreams
my fingers are stinkhorns and roots them out.
She throws away her gloves. She kisses
her own fingertips: they bloom, she waves them
at me, saying *And you think you know
so much about the future.*

She calls to her husband again
*Shut that damn thing off* thinking he'll disappear
into her voice if she talks loud enough
long enough. She peels off my face
but it's the wrong season. *You call* that *ripe?*
she asks, and plants me headfirst in the clay.
I hear the mower's vibrations. She shakes
my legs, my arms, complains of the poor soil.
*Men are all alike* the dream seems to say
and she nods vaguely, brushing an insect's hum
from her ear, already beginning to forget me.
*Go on down out of your body* she mumbles
*it's not my birthday.*
                        It's not her funeral
either. Her garden grows with no help
from the weather or my imagination;
all she has to do is keep dreaming
the right season and the suitable seed
and be careful to keep them separate.
*A good crop and nothing to regret* she says,
going right on whether I wake up or not.

 # THREE

## Plowing It Under

How is the darkness dark, or the light, light?
And how do we see by either the hand
Raised, or held out? When we give, do we uncage
Reasons for a new life, or ride again
Instinct, that tired horse, back to his stall?
                                    Does
Everything tend by nature toward the dumb fork
That says to us *One way or the other?*

Hard questions, if you take them seriously;
Only a fool ignores them, though, or a clod.
Do we bring form to the world, or does the world
Guide us through its maze? How will you know
Even if you find the true color, and your hand
Settles perfectly on its body, which is which?

## Casting

1

*Once upon a time* does well enough
to begin with, because the time went slow
then, an air we moved in,

a place to settle, like stones downward
in dark water, bottomless.
And how we drifted
                    —into each other's
slow motion, your brilliant hair awash,
disheveled on me; what distances
we brought together, all future there
in that loose light untangling, all
that waking
                    —into sons,
gifts of the first water, whose making
bore the simple
astonishment of parting
and again parting, the blind coming
becoming, not once but twice
                    —into this life,
a wholly imaginary vision

but the real thing, as all lives are wherein
no one lives happily ever after.

2

If it seems nothing much happened, it is
because we made no language for what happened,
made our experience everyone's experience,
believing without doubt or consciousness
we were immortal, which is to say

the whale of what we were and were doing
in the world swallowed us up.

3

Slow time
in that dark, slow motion, *I*
*love* I said *you*,
and you conceived sons.
                    I cut
a hole in the ice, sent my line down,
said *I love* of all people *you*
and you skated circles around me.
                        In the eye

of that tousled light I said nothing,
my empty mouth open, full of the sources
of speech, and you brought forth sons.

> I looked

at them, delicate, saw their names would be
*distance,* and said through it
*I love* and *you,*

> feeling in some blind depth

a stirring, which I struck gently,
gingerly, with furious restraint, and

hooked.

And let run, easing the drag. And run.

It runs still, no matter what
I bring to your table.

I remember that morning
when mornings were years, you came down
to the coffee and bacon whose smells
had wakened you, and I pointed
to three bass, gutted, on the drainboard.
I opened the wide mouth of one
wide enough to take in all Virginia,
and we opened ours.

Later to the sweetness still on my tongue,
to the feel of the taut line humming still
in my fingers, to you
still on my tongue, replete in the long morning,
I said

*I love.*

4

What can I say
to you now, Motherwife,
when ten years seem a day?
Can words, or words' echo,
release from this gathered life
an image of its needs,

as quick motion, or its shadow,
scatters the school from the reeds?

If they can, and if you could
see it and respond, how
would I know?
Though I still
sit at center ice
is that really you at play
on the far edges, teasing
my taut will?

If, in the devious
and poised tricks
of our sometime sex
—that slippery rage—
I can't make a match
fit for the mute turbulence
of this middle age,
must I go find some witch

who will teach me to brew
my life from old books,
and conjure, and construe,
and raise, if not the dead,
lost selves instead
to love, and grapple with
in the dustbed of myth:
i.e. turn to nothing worse

than the pitched depth of verse?
Nobody comes. Nobody
answers. I would say nothing's
left but to go down,
take a slow dive
to the poor dim bottom
where the mirrors live,
were it not pure tedium
there, without solace,

and crowded to boot. Malice,
like the many-humped serpent
of old maps, keeps watch

from his corner. I nod,
turn my back, decide
to hang on, play the fine catch
on this silly instrument
again. Silence, please,

this is my last reprise.

5

If it's a dream
only a person from the dream
can wake me.
                    No
one else is there.
                    I
hold the monofilament
at the lure's eye
suspended. A light
breaks upon it
a fine shower of gold.

Dazzled
        I
bend closer, my hand
misguiding, missing

such a simple act,
threading
the bait's eye.
                    I
continue to
fail
        seemingly forever
bowed
toward the shimmering brightness

blurred—so close,
now so many times

my mouth is
littered with hooks.

## Limbo for the Wedding of Divorce

1

Some woman,
badly impersonating my ex-wife,
entices my son up a hill.
They dance, laughing,
their blond hair flowing
currents in air.
                    At the foot of the hill
I turn my head
toward a chest I think full of silver
but see myself instead
as if I'm dreaming, close up:

I could fall into one of my own pores;
I could fall into my vacant smile.

2

One of my son's
teachers, badly disguised
as my ex-wife, is pulling him
away, above, laughing
echoes of light.
                I look
at the chest of silver she has
left for this wedding of divorce
and this time from a long distance
see myself looking down into it.

I cannot see what I see.

In the background the woman
and my son dance,

bright shadows.

3

The truth of the matter is, it *is*
my ex-wife, badly impersonating

herself, drawing my son
toward her, playing games.

The silver I never see shines
from the open chest, mixing its light
with the golden promise of the air.

They weren't meant for each other.

I want to give it all away.


## Ex-Wife

B. K. S.

The woman reading in the bathtub
holds the book in one hand,
keeping her place with her finger,
her arm drooping along the porcelain
toward the floor. She wipes the tip
of her nose with her other wrist, then turns
the tap briefly, adding water.

She has no story to tell. She has told me
so. She has only this tableau she gives
me through a crack in the blinds.
I lay the binoculars on the windowsill,
tip my head toward the bricks.
I don't know she will be dead in five years
but I wish I could help her. Hand her
the soap, take her riding in my tan car
by the river, meet her again coming
across the bridge on fire in her red scarf.

But it's been too long since she stepped
into the bathtub, leaving me
to scour the world for the book with two texts,
one lying transparently on the other
as if whispering to it,
opening secrets, filling the gaps.

Failure has brought me here. I lift the glasses
and look through the wrong end,
seeing her clearly
lean back in the bathtub, raise the book
and open it. Even at this distance,
she reads.


## The Top of the Forest

Simple adultery was how it started:
Always the body's wreck becomes its port;
Makeshift the world, piecemeal the living in it.
But the least chance will sometimes draw us in
Regardless our intentions: touch too well
And the lightest love becomes a gathering.

No place is how it finished, here at least.
Elsewhere what sweetness we let into the air
Edges toward music such as the deaf might make
Tuning the world, timing their losses in it.

 # FOUR

## The Innocent One's Last Words
## to the Guilty One

You will always be the one who did it.

I have told them so, because of my love for you,
but no one believes me. So
I have pretended I belong here
in your cell, the cell of our father,
that you might go free and repeat yourself
forever. I have made you

Immortal.

I will tell them a last time
*I am not the one, I do not deserve this,*
and when they hang me
it won't be the real thing.

The crowd will believe
the one dancing on the raw boards of the scaffold
beneath me is my shadow.

# What He Did with the New Egg

1   *He finds it too much to handle*

I reached into the mother's dry nest
and removed the new egg.
I cradled it in my arms looking
about, looking
about, and discovered a little thing
to do with it. But it was too large
to flush down the toilet.
I heaved it out the attic window
and watched it fall to the sidewalk;
it bounced a few times, didn't
break, just rolled into the grass.
It wouldn't fit into the saucepan.
I tried to stuff it back in
the nest, but it had outgrown that, too.

2   *So he imagines it small enough to hold in his hand*

I had such power over the future
I could have thrown it over the house,
or dunked it, or closed my hand
on it until it shattered into nothing.
But it rested so lightly on my palm,
so intent upon itself, my hand trembled.
I sat down.
I placed it on a table.
It glowed with my tenderness toward it.
An intricate pattern of blue tracery,
like veins under the skin,
began to show faintly through the shell.
I dipped a small brush
into little circles of color, and painted
the egg's design upon itself.

3   *He decides to let it be*

When its glow began to pulse
my eyes went slack;

I saw everything fade
and brighten,
fade and
brighten, in rhythm with my heartbeat.
At the same instant I collapsed
inward to the dot where I sat watching,
the egg exploded, its pieces spreading
in slow motion like an opening fan.
Where the egg had been my brother rises
in his life, throwing a ball
over and over in one graceful act
beyond prediction
toward his death, where he will catch it.

I put the egg back in the nest


## The Opposite Field
to my brother

1

An old photograph shows you
at two or three sitting in a puddle,
smiling, mud splattered
on your legs and shirt and face;
your arms, having swept through
the water, plunge skyward, filled,
I like to think now,
with your delight in simply being there.

Another from the same period of your life
shows you trying to drink from a garden hose,
the strong skyward arc
of water thwarting
you, your attention
immersed, your face
absolutely composed, without thirst.

In both photographs there is no future.

A figure of someone no less a stranger
emerges from these two images
the way vapor rises from Aladdin's lamp.
It takes shape, the features of its face
disposed to suggest your face, your light-
hearted summers mimicked in his gait, the crack
of the bat, sweet meat, the galling slide
into second, the earned bruise fading
into October, the mists of a possible life:

In the form this figure almost achieves
the shadows of your lost seasons call
to each other in the diamond dusk—
indecipherable voices, echoes,
and I imagine you turning in your bed
touched vaguely beneath the familiar
nightmares which have become mere aspects
of your sleep, touched so far
back, so close to what you wanted
to be, then, now,
it's as if I said, *Brother,*
*here we are again:*

*Catch.*

2

June, 1981. You are forty.
*Il se situe par rapport au temps:*
We will have to follow *that* curve to its end.

3

I had not thought to find
you so bound,
so driven into the wood.

In the sour locker rooms
we both remember—stretching
their dim tunnels from the first
wet practice all the way

to marriage—some dog
would have said, *'Smatter, lost
your balls?*

        and you would have conned
him so casually, with such play—
the whole team watching—
he'd have thought you wanted
to borrow his.
        Instead,
in the thick heat of Houston,
on real grass, under a glazed dome
of sky and no one watching,
you fungo flies to your son,
to me. The thin *tick* of the wood
on the ball rehearses
itself endlessly, routine
grounder, routine pop-up, big
out *tick* routine:
           after an hour
I take the bat, wave you deep
down the green reaches, stroking
them high and long, driving
you to the wall again
and again, up against it time
after time, and then *over*
the wall, Lord, into the next
field,
    farther,
        the next season,
until I don't know where
you are, have never known . . .
           wanting
your will and heart to keep
from breaking—impossible—
your release into the fabulous spaces.

4   *A Lyric Meditation on Sour Locker Rooms*

Almost always underground, dank,
at least one corner stinking of piss;

31

pasty men in cages, doling; bodies
being numbered, uniformed, strapped—
dogsbodies, Dog days, even in mild April.

                                  Can you go up
from this cavern of mock cells, single file,
into the blare of the green field,
virgin again, lined, and can you
remember how to come back down, the place
empty with you in it, alone, benched, cracked
in bone and will, soaked in your own sweat,
the concrete damp under your bare feet, steamed,
and no shower quite able to drown
the echoes of the metal door opening,
closing,
              the crowd stunned by the high arc
of the ball hung in the glare, against the dark.

5

Am I brother to you
the same way I am friend
to the scattered few
people who have woven
together with me, me
and themselves: I mean, through
such distance in time
and space that the cloth
of our love seems to stretch
into transparency,
the very air of our breath,
a net so thin it may be
impossible to catch
us, no matter how far we fall?
                         Hard
brotherhood.
              I prefer the sweet arc
of the batted ball, grave
and graceful at once, curving
upward and out, downward and in,
to the enfolding glove.

6

A newer photograph shows you
and me it's not a game, this life.

The camera arrests neither motion
nor implicit gesture, you are simply

all there is, you
and the background of stones,

shadowed—your face, the lines
in your forehead. Your hair

recedes. No one needs to tell you
ghosts share your sleep.

Sometime after the shutter clicks
you probably put on your shirt,

stand up, and walk
toward home. The image

of your possible life
watches from a distance. Fading,

he picks up a pebble
and tosses it aside, lightly. The sound

of its landing becomes
our purest dream.

## Family Life

Most of this life gets talked almost to death,
All the lines of attraction, fields of force,
Reticulate lashings of father and son,
Son and father, death and the maidenhead.
Help we don't get, probably because we shouldn't;
After Janus the future finishes with us,
Leaving the mesh clogged with our dumb complaints,
Language of the kind we long for might let us say

How little love has to do with survival.

Still, we love our children and attend their needs,
Tell them old stories about the magic weaver
Unfolding truth and rescue as one tapestry,
As they in their turn try out that play and this,
Rehearsing each role as if it were a skin,
Teaching us not to believe it, but to accept.

 **FIVE**

## When We Have Crossed Over

When we have crossed over into Franz Kafka
we won't find new bread to eat,
we won't discover a perfect language
all of whose words are essential to our lives.

The pinched end of the funnel
through which the world has always dumped itself
into us will not widen
and release the waste and the ghosts,

the professor will not give us a good grade,

nothing will dawn,
nothing will be burned away,
nothing will happen

except the gross net through which
we have let the nuggets of our sorrow fall
will become a mesh finer than the eye of God
which seines everything.

## Riding Amtrak Through Southwest Texas

Dry wash, silt
riverbed, clipped hills;

a stunted tree: I feel myself
a curt branch of it;

         almost
dead at forty, worth my weight
in water, I look
out on the dry land
and find it dry:

        a cap
of stones on a mound of stones,
a corona; everywhere
the blank plain; once,
a windmill, sheep.

        The whole
a periodic repetition—
            I have
been set down in a wide throat,
father; what I know
might swallow me
were I not so astonished
to find it, to find it
has always been there
            —almost
a sentence.


## Winter Letter to My Son at Fourteen

I saw my mother, at seventy-one, step down
her footprints in the snow, like stairs.

I saw myself as a child bound
in mittens squatting in the snow.

I saw your brother's foot poking
up out of the snow he'd fallen into.

This happened before you were born.
This happened today.


## The Birds

> Who can know what all his
> mortalities are?
> —Farad Karaji

1

                        That midwinter day
you could almost
say the sandpipers ambled, hungry,
their bright eyes cocked
toward the minute pores glinting
in the sand—
            ambled
almost,
        but when the next wave broke
and spread toward them
they broke, too, sprinting
back up the beach, break-
neck, their brittle legs flailing
like pendulums gone mad.

They always outran the sea,
but they seemed barely to touch it, too,
to keep no distance; it was as if
they drew each wave in after them,
not fleeing at all, and then followed it
back as it withdrew: one motion,

bird and water, water
and bird, serene,
a paradigm.

2

                      Sometimes in the dead
middle of the night when the knot
under my sternum tightens and presses upward
as though it would part my rib cage
and hatch itself,
I place the forefinger of one hand
on the thin vein winging my other wrist
and feel beat there my father's
puzzled belief that a life is always edging
toward itself, that if enough be done,
be gotten through, today, then tomorrow a man's
dream of himself might settle down
out of the distant air onto his shoulder,
flutter its wings a little, and at last
rest,

that such success would take the place of death,
of history, of time.
              I touch my wrist: his
life
goes on, it goes
on; I am unsettled, too,
by this conviction, that one day
my imagination will draw all
that it releases
back into itself.

3

Sandpiper, killdeer, mourning dove, quail,
how can you fly with a salted tail?

*Ask the old crow on the split rail*

Rock bird, water bird, bird of woe,
what do you eat in the spring snow?

*Ask the crow*

When your craw is empty, how do you sing?
Can you make shift with a cracked wing?

*The crow knows everything*

When you can't manage a stiff wind
what shelter do you find?

*The crow's kind*

Dry bird, broken bird, bird of gray,
how do you get through a bad day?

*The crow's way*

Birds of my life,

birds of my air, my song's mouth,
what are your answers worth?
Give me the practical truth.

*You don't fool us with your litany*
*You don't wonder what, how, why*
*You want to know how to die*

*Look in the crow's eye.*

4

One-a-penny, two-a-penny, they settled
like flakes of air:

ducks on the pond.

When Remington-Peters set my father in the blind
once a year in the prime of the season
he never hit anything.
He never hit anything
when they set him in the field, either
with the best dogs pointing,

the startled quail whirring
upward from the hedges.
                                    When he
aimed from the blind, or raised
his dull gun in the dull day
to the flushed covey,
                            the birds flew
on the blank surface of his glasses,

free there,

like he is, here.

5

It's ten o'clock in April again. It's snowing.
Nine years ago today two killdeer courted
my first son into the world: their incredible wings

will bend within his wrists as long as he lives. Blood
brothers. We are in Athens, Ohio;
everyone's cellar is filling with water, maybe

in celebration of my father's grandson's turning
into his tenth year in the mixed seasons
filling the city with spring snow, spring flood;

it seems such pressure could unmoor it
and send it floating over the Appalachians seaward
into West Virginia; the light would fly up

out of the pine trees, startled, flocking.
If it veered northward
we might understand

that all along it has been a migration like this
the mourning doves wonder about out loud.
Even now they call toward the lost light.

In such a time, in April, you could almost imagine
a child standing under the pines,
shadowed. He could lift his hand to them

and open it, releasing among their needles
an affable light, a flying instant
which might nest in them, a birthday covenant

of the impossible flight.


## Because Nothing

1

Nuclear vision suggests that a curious man
Ask his first question only if he is willing
To ask the next one, and the next, *et cetera*,
Holding tightly to nothing, because nothing is
All we get, whatever its shape. This life
Never gives up its secrets to a humorless man.

2

Very soon after     the semblances departed
Our rivers swelled with new water     we relaxed
Nobody noticed our     shadows too     had departed

*So what* some said     inventing fine weapons
*Can we help     the solidity of the world?*
Happiness seemed possible once     again
In dark cellars     the roots of the future grew
Little by little     everything settled     down
Last of all the rivers dried up the sky     lowered
In time     no one remembered anything
*Now we are free*     some said shriveling
Giving this plea to their mirrors     *Clear     Clear*

3

Sometimes you feel like you're the only one in the world.
Those are hard times because they're true, partly.
Until you learn to live with them, you can't live;

And after you learn, you may have to learn again.
Remember, forget; collect, cast away; continue.
Tomorrow is no beginning, nor ending, but another day.


## Patrimony


Arriving home in the evening
I call out, "Who's the best?"

She answers, "We're the best,"
and slides into my arms.

The offspring of our coming together
will find his blood so rich with love

he will have to kill me,
drag my body to the sweet river flowing

near our town and dump me in.
I will be so happy for him

I will sing while I float all the way
to the river's mouth, and he will walk home

absorbing the melody, the words.
I can hear him learning

them so well it seems nothing
has happened. He walks

toward home humming neither regret
nor doubt, humming absently nothing

has happened. There's no one
to warn him, he doesn't listen

when the shiftless vagrant whispers
to him as he starts toward his door,

"Walk on by," nothing for it
but to come in humming absently

my song, the song of love and truth
his mother echoes, welcoming with a kiss.


## Listening


Diamond and vinyl's an unlikely combination
And yet the insensible needle
Renders music from the mute grooves,
Real revolution. Your intricate, fine-tuned
Ear is no less rare, measuring
Nothing as it rises into the air.

When you make music
You sometimes touch such untold parts of yourself,
Near the edges of everybody's time, that all sounds
New again, as it can in our first hearing.
Even Winter listens, and plans to blossom.

Singing's darkest seasons can
Tease us into beginning, too, if we want;
Unless the beautiful changes, you'll have to coax it
Again and again out of the world's cold deafness,
Releasing airs in
To the settling air.

## God

lives
as a man who loses a son
lives

 # SIX

## Crib Death

Kisses are for the living.
Even if the terrible breath of the dead
Never rose from the earth's mouth,
Dread of it would turn our heads aside
As relatives at a funeral meet and kiss.
Living in such air is what the living have,
Less choice than a stone what's cut into its face.

## Traces of a Bicameral Mind

1   *One Way*

What will I remember,
dying? What will I kiss?
Will it be the same mouth?

I know that after we have looked into the dark
long enough it seems we are blind
and not simply looking at darkness.

Whatever looks back at me, it is
not myself, nor the years of this making,
nor my furtive wish to have done with it.

The mouth of my life.

2 *Night Air*

I know that after we have looked into the dark
long enough it seems we are blind
and not simply looking at darkness.
Nobody's eyes adjust. We realize at last
we are surrounded. It's dark now

and if I should speak through my blindness,
fine particles of sound, a kind of dust,
would enter the dark,
not as a man enters a woman,
but as air enters the lungs
of creatures, breathing.

The darkness would change them
into something no one could recognize,
or trace,

not as the zygote couldn't recognize
the egg, the sperm, or so improbable a joining,

but as a crazed man who hears
in his ear, which is the ear of the world,
a thickness he cannot touch
growing, might ask

*What is this which devours me?*

## Don't Look Back

1

I walk through the high-ceilinged
yesterday of forever. Nobody's
in there who's supposed to be.
I want the legend
of bubbling glasses and happy people

in all the rooms, family
like I dreamed of when the real people
were there with their fake cheer.
I want them to be mine,
their warmth to lift me into the domes
with the other angels.
I laugh, and it's still
all gone, an empty never.

2

In one party room the yesterday
people clutter, I
stumble on a rug. *Don't
just lie there* an uncle says
and sits on my chest,
*Get something up.* Everyone
lifts their glasses and pours
ice cubes on my groin:
*To your future sons* they call out,
*May they rise and rise
until you are just a man
lying on a rug in an empty
gone.* Like I am.
It would be enough if someone,
any ghost, would come
and sit in the window.
He could say something, or not,
just being,
and I could breathe deeply
and let it all out.

3

Or in the kitchen where the black women
wear gardenias
in their hair
and hum to the kettle.
The steam makes little beads
of water quiver
on the ceiling. And such food!

47

Even the desperate people
who live in their 100-proof
glasses grow tame eating it.
It's all gone, I lie
on the rug under the table
listening for the lost voices
of the black women
murmuring as they clear.


## The Old Figure


When I come before the old figure of judgment
to tell him my miracle
we will be all the same:

he with his veil of light, I
carrying the wings in my hands,
the miracle waiting
to be delivered up from our dream.

He knows where the memories are;
he calls them *Father*.
With a gesture of blessing
he undoes my chest
and releases them all.
They fly off, their wings
making a sound like laughter.

When I look at him again
it is his laughter. I want
to give him my lightened heart,
my life, be shut of everything,

but he climbs through the hole in my chest
and sews it up from the inside.

## Discovering My Daughter

Most of your life we have kept our separate places:
After I left your mother you knew an island,
Rented rooms, a slow coastal slide northward
To Boston, and, in summer, another island
Hung at the country's tip. Would you have kept going
All the way off the map, an absolute alien?

Sometimes I shiver, being almost forgetful enough
To have let that happen. We've come the longer way
Under such pressure, from one person to ⸜
Another. Our trip proves again the world is
Round, a singular island where people may come
Together, as we have, making a singular place.

## The Girl of My Dreams Is Dying

I bend over her but she waves
me off. *I don't need you
anymore* she says. *This is no time
to fool around* I tell her.
*This is death.* I try to take
her hand, all I want
is to comfort her, but she jerks
it away. She tries to cup
her breasts and thrust them
toward me but her fists
knot the blanket
where her chest used to be. *Lose
something?* I ask.
*Your future* she says and spits
five or six teeth at me.
They settle to the floor
like milkweed. A small writhing
happens vaguely under the covers.
I lean down again

and take in my arms all
that's left of her, a hint
of eucalyptus and mint, the sweetest
echo of nothing I've ever heard.


## This Is No Dream, This Is My Life


1

I am Humphrey Bogart.

I can do
anything.

I can take the wheel.

I can ride
the wild lust of a flame-haired woman
morning to morning,

smoke two packs
of nonfiltered cigarettes
a day,

fly.

I can
not give a damn.

I can go into my private
room, sit on the bed
and put my feet in my ears,

or sit at the window
and watch myself walk away into the mountains
forever, never
looking back,

until I am nothing
except the spoor
draining from my left heel,
following me.

Hot shit.

2

The mountains into which Humphrey Bogart
walked
are so clear this morning
it could break your heart.

Steaming slightly, his trail
could be the collected neuroses
of the Western world
since Paul's first letter to the Corinthians,
dropped finally in the chill air.

You could imagine him,
a new wind grazing his face,
done forever with the badlands
air filled with mustard and dry ice.

He might turn around near the top
and flick his cigarette toward you,
smile his enigmatic smile
as if to say, "I'm all you've got
and now I'm gone," so clear

in the chill air of the morning
it could break your heart.

3

Even at this distance I can see
the pines
on the mountain where Bogey disappeared
ripple in the wind.

Empty of everything
else, I swell with such longing
I could join Macy's Thanksgiving parade
in midair, like Mighty Mouse.

Inflated thus, a growing pain,
I float out the window.
When I come to the mountains
I hover, feeling
*This must be it, this must be*
*the one she promised*
*to be.* And slowly come
down
into the heaving pines.

The explosion should be the end
of me, more nothing,
but instead I hear a voice
I take to be Bogey's, whispering
*Leave the old bag to me*
and find myself walking down
the mountain, my feet bare against the dirt,
not looking back.

## Snapshots of the Writer Entering Middle Age

### 1

The first one shows him in a room
with nothing to hide. A clock
is turned toward the wall, and the wall
toward it, a meeting from which arises
a semblance of fire, the finest of shadows,
where reflections of his faces shimmer.
He seems to throw water on it with one hand,
and with the other, fanning, to feed it air.

### 2

He was caught often with his mouth open
but this time his astonishment seems
drier than usual, less rehearsed,
as if he had looked obliquely past the log
he is splitting and the habitual axe,
made alien by inattention, shied off the wood,
fell into his shin instead, and he saw the bone.

### 3

In this double exposure
he appears a shadow of himself:
through his transparent rib cage you can see
a meadowlark, the black V striking
its yellow throat, perched on a high-tension wire
which, an inch or so to the bird's left, simply
stops, releasing its current
into the ribbed air, the airless photograph,
where he and the bird are breathing.